Questions for Students

A Practical Guide for Journal Writing and Discussions

By Joe Deely

NEW FORUMS

NEW FORUMS PRESS INC.

Published in the United States of America
by New Forums Press, Inc.1018 S. Lewis St.
Stillwater, OK 74074
www.newforums.com

Library of Congress Cataloging-in-Publication Data Pending

This book may be ordered in bulk quantities at discount from New
Forums Press, Inc., P.O. Box 876, Stillwater, OK 74076 [Federal
I.D. No. 73 1123239]. Printed in the United States of America.

ISBN 10: 1-58107-327-5
ISBN 13: 978-1-58107-327-0

Testimonials

"In a day and age where social media and video games rule the minds of teens and young adults alike.......this book, *Questions for Students,* is refreshing and inspiring. It provides a platform for students to read, think about, and respond to a vast array of questions posed to them in a safe environment where they can be open and honest with their responses. Mr. Deely, a friend and colleague of mine, uses this form of journaling to reach students who may or may not want to be 'reached'. He uses these questions to open a dialogue with students who aren't a true fan of the traditional educational system and as a result is able to create a bond with his students to further their educational endeavors without them (the students) even realizing what he has done. Mr. Deely, an excellent educator, who is known for making connections with young minds who need a role model that thinks outside of the box by posing just the right question."

Mary Lisker
High School Transition Coordinator

"Joe Deely's *Questions for Students (A Practical Guide for Journal Writing and Discussions)* is a go-to resource for any educator or parent of a teen looking to encourage self-reflection and deeper thinking. The questions are relevant and challenging, prompting adolescents to reflect on situations surrounding their daily lives and future goals. As a high school assistant principal and the parent of two teens, *Questions for Students* truly is a practical guide for connecting with teens and providing them with opportunities to better understand themselves through journal writing and discussions."

Michelle Martin
M.Ed., High School Assistant Principal

"The book, *Questions for Students (A Practical Guide for Journal Writing and Discussions),* is a great tool for any teacher or parent's belt. The material is down to earth and realistic. It is easy to interpret and apply to real life situations. As a teacher I am looking forward to using this in my classroom to prepare my students for their future."

Chris Garland
Special Education Teacher/Case Manager

"Joe Deely offers fellow teachers a guide to help students develop their thoughts over hundreds of topics. The use of open-ended questions to stimulate careful thinking encourages students to put their feelings into words, letting them express and enhance the thought process. I am very impressed with his approach and believe that it has the potential to build insight and self-awareness. I highly recommend this inspiring instrument of education."

Dave Ridenour
Retired Public School Teacher

"Being a teenager is hard. There's a lot to process and navigate. Making students take the time to actually deliberate on their thoughts and put them down on paper will help kids to be better peers and to make better decisions. I wish a teacher had assigned me some of Mr. Deely's writing prompts".

Christian J. Cotz
Director of Education and Visitor Engagement
James Madison's Montpelier

"Time and again, Mr. Deely offers insightful information during data meetings about our students. When everyone asked him to explain his secret for knowing what may be impacting a student, he smiled and stated he learned the information from reading responses to these writing prompts. These interesting and diverse prompts work! Enjoy!"

John Ringstaff
Assistant High School Principal

"I can't say enough about the wonderful variety and allure of the questions that Joe Deely presents to his students. What's good about these questions is students can be engaged first in meaningful discussions, and then back it up with writing. It's a great tool for reluctant writers."

Mark Hopkins
M.A.Ed., Special Education Teacher,
New York State

Table of Contents

Introduction.. 1
Applications 3
Thoughts of Others 5

Section 1 - Questions for the beginning of school year 7
Section summary.. 8
1. AAA.. 9
2. First few days.. 9
3. Good advice to students... 9
4. Lessons of life... 9
5. New semester goals 10
6. Parent pride... 10
7. Positive attitude 10
8. Summer fun 10

Section 2 - Questions about general topics 11
Section summary 12
1. Animal fear 15
2. Attention 15
3. Bed time... 15
4. Being cool... 15
5. Being nice 16
6. Best dream 16
7. Best quality 16
8. Birthday 16
9. Breaking up.. 17
10. Cell phones 17
11. Complaining 17
12. Cooking 17
13. Depression 18
14. Do not like 18

15. Drugs 18
16. Economy 18
17. Fashion 19
18. Fast food 19
19. Fat 19
20. Fear 19
21. Fire 20
22. Freedom 20
23. Frightened 20
24. Frustration 20
25. Fun 21
26. Games 21
27. Gangs 21
28. Get a job 21
29. Getting fit 22
30. Getting older (positives) 22
31. Getting older (negatives) 22
32. Gift 22
33. Going to California 23
34. Going to die 23
35. Growing up 23
36. Jail 23
37. Job 24
38. Judge 24
39. Life 24
40. Like me 24
41. Live without 24
42. Love 25
43. Make a difference 25
44. Marijuana 25
45. Me 25
46. Money 26
47. Nice to hear 26
48. No one cares 26
49. Occupation 26
50. Opposite sex 27
51. Pet peeve 27

52. Pet 27
53. Police 27
54. Poor 28
55. Popular music 28
56. Popularity 28
57. Positive role model 28
58. Possession 29
59. Pride 29
60. Regret 29
61. Religion 29
62. Season 30
63. Sick or hurt 30
64. Sleep 30
65. Smell 30
66. Space 31
67. Sports or business 31
68. STD 31
69. Stress 31
70. Stupid choices 32
71. Success 32
72. Teens working 32
73. Temper 32
74. Top ten things to do before you die 33
75. True hero 33
76. TV show 33
77. TV viewing 33
78. Vandalism 34
79. Video games 34
80. What you don't Know can't hurt you 34
81. Who 34
82. Worst qualities 35

Section 3 – Questions concerning home and family 37
Section summary 38
1. Adoption 39
2. Advice about parents 39
3. Bad parent 39

4. Best vacation...39
5. Child abuse 40
6. Curfews 40
7. Funny thing...40
8. Good advice to parent...40
9. Good parent 41
10. Ideal weekend...41
11. Living with frustration..41
12. Old argument..41
13. Spoiled brat..42
14. Tell parent..42
15. Weekend 42
16. Where are you from?...42

Section 4 - Questions that pose dilemmas....................43
Section summary 44
1. Animals..45
2. Blame 45
3. Car Not Starting..45
4. Corporal Punishment 45
5. Crash...46
6. Dead..46
7. Death Penalty..46
8. Drinking Age 46
9. Energy Drinks...47
10. Faces...47
11. Free 47
12. Gun 47
13. Job Choices..48
14. Lost Money...48
15. Make A Wish 48
16. Mind Or Body 49
17. Operation 49
18. Philanthropy 49
19. Restroom find 49
20. Robbery 50
21. Soap Opera 50

22. Theft 50
23. View A Crime 51
24. Wallet 51
25. Wrong Change 51
26. Your Choice 52

Section 5 – Questions that are school related 53
Section summary 54
1. Advice to friend 55
2. Boys or girls 55
3. Diploma 55
4. Don't get it 56
5. Failure 56
6. Favorite class 56
7. My rules 56
8. No school 57
9. Pick your teacher 57
10. School learning 57
11. School subject 57
12. School uniforms 58
13. Secret 58
14. Senior 58
15. Snacks and sodas 58
16. Snow days 59
17. Teacher 59
18. Graduate 59

Section 6 - Questions that are fantasies 61
Section summary 62
1. 10 Years 64
2. 100 64
3. Army 64
4. Big adventure 64
5. Big storm 65
6. Big talk 65
7. Blind 65
8. Cat 66

9. Celebrity interest.. 66
10. Change... 66
11. Choices 66
12. Different look 67
13. Dinner time.. 67
14. Dream house.. 67
15. Dream machine.. 67
16. England.. 68
17. Go anywhere.. 68
18. Heads up.. 68
19. Helping out.. 68
20. Invisible 69
21. Last meal 69
22. Movie star.. 69
23. Murder 69
24. Musical instrument.. 70
25. New job 70
26. New parent 70
27. New way... 70
28. No diseases 71
29. No money 71
30. No parents.. 71
31. Olympic fall... 71
32. One month 72
33. One wish.. 72
34. Other shoe.. 72
35. Out to eat 72
36. Rich 73
37. Sing, sing, sing 73
38. Star... 73
39. Stuck.. 73
40. Time machine 74
41. Which one.. 74

Section 7 - Questions during holidays or big events 75
Section summary 76
 1ˢᵗ Quarter.. 77

1. Earth Day 77
2. Flu season 77
3. Halloween 77
4. Love is great 78
5. Love stinks... 78
6. New year – New you 78
7. New Year's resolutions 78
8. New Year 79
9. Reflections 79
10. Spring break 79
11. Spring... 79
12. Super Bowl 80
13. Thankful 80
14. Time change 80
15. Vote... 80
16. Wild turkey 81
17. Winter break fun.. 81
18. Winter break 81

Section 8 - Questions for the end of the school year 83
Section summary... 84
1. 9 to go 85
2. Final pull.. 85
3. Goals for next year 85
4. Next year.. 85
5. Looking back 86
6. Summer plans 86

Closing Thoughts 87
Acknowledgements.. 89
About the Author... 91

Introduction

I have found that most questions seldom have definitive answers. Children, and often quite a few adults, like to have answers to their questions that are solved with clear-cut and easy to grasp responses. Unfortunately, clearly defined black and white answers are seldom accurate and I have often been suspect of responses to questions when I am given quick and assured answers. Our minds have a tendency to want ideas and concepts to be deconstructed so they may be easily pigeon-holed into understandable categories to make them simple to digest.

Some of the most fundamental questions should raise the most difficult and more complex responses, yet we seemed to have evolved into a species that desires immediate satisfactions. Answers to questions without the understandings of solutions will cause us to slip into an unreasoning and thoughtless society where logic and meditation have faded away. Asking questions and constructing ways to address the problems they pose is one of the keys to our development as a culture.

Kids need to have their thoughts challenged. As they develop they should be stirred repeatedly by questions that evoke thoughts and reactions. It can be argued that our ability to use reason to sort through complex questions is what separates us from other animals. Questioning our surroundings is perhaps our best avenue that can inspire truth and creativity, thus enhancing our ability to advance the evolution of our minds.

J.D.

Applications

These are the questions I pose to my students for their daily writing journals. Getting my students to write at the start of class has been a great way to begin my time with them because it immediately involves them in a short activity that engages their minds and produces work. Students earn full credit if they address the questions and give support of their answers in their responses. For feedback I'll point out writing errors and give suggestions and comments of support.

Through their responses I see their strength and weaknesses as writers and find the areas they need to work on, but often, and perhaps more importantly, it gives me insight on issues my students are dealing with. Students will often confide in their journals topics they are unable or unwilling to vocalize. The journal questions have been a great way to cut through many issues both academically and emotionally that students face each day. This helps with building relationships that ultimately results in trust, which typically manifests into them producing quality work.

These prompts will often inspire discussions about key issues of the day which are a great way to make important connections with my students. Through developing these personal connections it has enabled me to know my students better and to teach to them at their levels. I use these questions as tools that I think other teachers can easily implement in their classroom. Hopefully teachers from a variety of academic levels will find this book useful and can create writing and discussion lessons based on these questions.

Parents might find this book a fun way to discover what their children are thinking about and how they use reason and logic to arrive at answers. See where these questions might take you and above all enjoy what you discover and have good time mulling through the possibilities. I hope the questions in this book inspire deeper thinking and contemplative reflections; things which humanity needs more than ever.

J.D.

Thoughts of Others

"The important thing is not to stop questioning. Curiosity has its own reason for existing."
Albert Einstein

"Did I offer peace today? Did I bring a smile to someone's face? Did I say words of healing? Did I let go of my anger and resentment? Did I forgive? Did I love? These are the real questions. I must trust that the little bit of love that I sow now will bear many fruits, here in this world and the life to come."
Henri Nouwen

"No one is dumb who is curious. The people who don't ask questions remain clueless throughout their lives."
Neil deGrasse Tyson

"I think that's the single best piece of advice: constantly think about how you could be doing things better and questioning yourself."
Elon Musk

Questions for the beginning of the school year

At the beginning of each school year I give my students writing prompts to help them think in terms of what it might be like to be a successful student. Often students who find themselves in my classroom have had difficulties in the past doing well at school. It is my hope that these questions they see the first few weeks of the school year will inspire them to think in terms of what it would be like to be a good student, and what efforts it will take to get them to that point. These are not the more thought provoking questions that they will later be exposed to, but rather questions that hopefully will start them off on their yearlong journal entries with success.

> **"Being a humble and down to earth person would make them proud."**
> *A line from a student's response to # 6 - "Parent Pride"*

Questions for the beginning of school year

1. AAA
2. First few days
3. Good advice to students
4. Lessons of life
5. New semester goals
6. Parent pride
7. Positive attitude
8. Summer fun

1 "AAA"

How would your life be different if you got straight A's and always did well in school? How would your family and teachers react? Make sure to explain how this would make you feel.

2 "First Few Days"

Congratulations! You have made it through the first few days of this semester. What positive things have already happened? What classes do you already like? Explain why you like the classes you picked.

3 "Good Advice for a New Student"

What good advice would you give a new student coming to school this year? Make sure to fully explain and defend your advice by giving examples.

4 "Lesson of Life"

What do you think was the most important lesson you learned in school last year? What do you hope to learn more about this year? Make sure to be specific in your explanation.

5 "New Semester Goals"

Please number your paper 1-5 and list 5 goals you want to achieve by the end of this semester. These goals can be both academic and personal. Make sure the goals you pick can be achieved.

6 "Parent Pride"

What type of things could you do with your life that would make your parents proud of your accomplishment? What type of person do you think you could be that would make them happy? Make sure to be specific in your response.

7 "Positive Attitude"

How can having a positive attitude help you do well in school? Make sure to explain your answer.

8 "Summer Fun"

What is something you did this past summer that was fun? Did you go anywhere? Make sure to fully explain your response.

Questions about general topics

This section covers the largest range of topics included in this book. These questions are geared towards issues that students can relate to or have some prior knowledge of. As with any section in this book I will not use every question each school year. I may omit or slightly change some of the questions depending on the dynamics of a class, with consideration to any issues some students may be having. Every school year is different with changes happening both internally within a school and externally in the larger world picture. It is always good to be flexible and have questions that can be modified to fit the appropriate situations for the students.

"Something that ticks me off more than anything would be when people tell me I can't do something. I'm not really sure why this makes me upset."

Lines from a student's response to #51 - "Pet Peeve"

Questions about general topics

1. Animal fear
2. Attention
3. Bed time
4. Being cool
5. Being nice
6. Best dream
7. Best quality
8. Birthday
9. Breaking up
10. Cell phones
11. Complaining
12. Cooking
13. Depression
14. Do not like
15. Drugs
16. Economy
17. Fashion
18. Fast food
19. Fat
20. Fear
21. Fire
22. Freedom
23. Frightened
24. Frustration
25. Fun
26. Games
27. Gangs
28. Get a job

29. Getting fit
30. Getting older (positives)
31. Getting older (negatives)
32. Gift
33. Going to California
34. Going to die
35. Growing up
36. Jail
37. Job
38. Judge
39. Life
40. Like me
41. Live without
42. Love
43. Make a difference
44. Marijuana
45. Me
46. Money
47. Nice to hear
48. No one cares
49. Occupation
50. Opposite sex
51. Pet peeve
52. Pet
53. Police
54. Poor
55. Popular music
56. Popularity
57. Positive role model
58. Possession
59. Pride
60. Regret
61. Religion
62. Season

63. Sick or hurt
64. Sleep
65. Smell
66. Space
67. Sports or business
68. STD
69. Stress
70. Stupid choices
71. Success
72. Teens working
73. Temper
74. Top ten things to do before you die
75. True hero
76. TV show
77. TV viewing
78. Vandalism
79. Video games
80. What you don't know can't hurt you
81. Who
82. Worst qualities

1 "Animal fear"

What animal or insect do you fear or are intimidated by the most? Have you ever been near this type of creature? Make sure to explain why it is you are afraid of this creature.

2 "Attention"

Why do you think some people need more attention than others? Do you require a lot of attention? Who do you like to get attention from? Make sure to explain your response.

3 "Bed time"

Do you think that having a bed time for teens is a good idea? What do you think is an appropriate bed time for someone your age? Make sure to defend and explain your opinion in your response.

4 "Being cool"

Many students in school spend a lot of energy trying to be cool and fit in. Why do you think it is so important for some students to think they are cool? What does it mean to be cool? Are you cool? Make sure to explain your response.

5 "Being nice"

What does it cost a person to be nice to others? Have you ever caught yourself being mean when you could have been nice? Why do you think it is better to be a kind person than a difficult one? Make sure to explain your response.

6 "Best dream"

Describe the best dream you ever had. Why do you think this one has stuck in your memory? Make sure to explain your response.

7 "Best qualities"

Each of us have qualities about our personality that make up who we are. What are the qualities about you that are the best? Are you nice, honest, and caring? What qualities about you are your strengths? Make sure to explain.

8 "Birthdays"

We all have them. When is your birthday and how old will you be then? What do you most look forward to about your next birthday? Do you think you'll ever get tired of having birthdays? Make sure to explain your response.

9 "Breaking up"

What do you think is the best way to break up with someone you care about? Give an example of how you think a break up should happen where no one gets hurt.

10 "Cell phones"

How has the development of the cell phone changed our lives? How do you think cell phones may negatively affect the minds of young people? Make sure to explain your response.

11 "Complaining"

Many people complain about things but they never do anything to change their situation. Why do you think so many people complain about stuff but they never do anything to help change things? Make sure to explain your response.

12 "Cooking"

What is something you make to eat that is good? Do you have a culinary specialty that others enjoy? This might be a main dish or a side. This may even be a type of dessert. Make sure to explain your response.

13 "Depression"

Fact: Everyone gets depressed from time to time. What are the things in your life that bum you out the most? How do you cope when you are feeling down? Make sure to be specific by giving examples.

14 "Don't like"

How do you deal with people you don't like? What is the best strategy you can use to keep from getting into arguments with people you just can't get along with? Make sure to explain your response.

15 "Drugs"

Why do you think some people take and abuse both legal and illegal drugs? How do you think this may negatively affect the minds of students? Make sure to explain your response.

16 "Economy"

Our economy is not doing so well. What would you do if you had the power to change things to help the economy? How would you go about giving help to individual families? Make sure to explain your response.

---

17 "Fashion"

Why is fashion so important to some people? How is what you wear important to you? Make sure to explain your response.

18 "Fast food"

Explain why you think fast food restaurants are so popular. Do you eat at these places? How do you think eating fast food may have a negative impact on you? Make sure to explain your response.

19 "Fat"

Fact: American teenagers are more overweight than ever before. Why do you think that teenagers are tipping the scales? What might help change this trend? Make sure to explain your response.

20 "Fear"

What is one of your greatest fears? Why do you think you are you afraid of this? Make sure to explain your response.

21 "Fire!"

You get woken up at 3:17 in the morning by someone yelling, "FIRE!" What will you do? Make sure to specifically explain your actions in this situation.

22 "Freedom"

Here in the United States we use the term freedom a lot. Do we have freedom in this country, or is it just word a politicians like to use? Make sure to defend your point of view by giving support in your explanation.

23 "Frightened"

Have you ever been really scared or frightened? Describe a time when you have been afraid. Make sure to explain your response.

24 "Frustration"

What do you find to be the most frustrating thing in your life? Things like school, teachers, siblings, parents, etc. can all cause us to get annoyed and frustrated. What gets you the most frustrated? Make sure to be specific in your response.

25 "Fun"

What would you do if you wanted to have a weekend of just pure fun? Who would you want to hang out with? Make sure to explain why these activities are fun for you in your response.

26 "Games"

Humans have been playing games for centuries. What are your three favorite games? These can be physical, board, or computer games. Be specific and explain the reasons why you like the games you picked.

27 "Gangs"

Why do gangs exist? Why do you think that so many young people fall into the trap of being in a gang? How can you avoid being in a gang? Make sure to be specific in your response.

28 "Get a job"

If you wanted to get a job at a local grocery store what are some of the things you could do to get hired? Think of the many things that go into getting yourself prepared to be selected for this job. Make sure to explain in your response.

29 "Getting fit"

If you wanted to get into the best shape possible what would be your goals towards wellness? Make sure to be specific in your explanation.

30 "Getting older - negative"

We're all getting older. What do you consider the worst part about getting older? What type of things do you not look forward to about being older? Make sure to explain your response.

31 "Getting older - positive"

We're all getting older. What do you consider the best part about getting older? What type of things do you look forward to about being older? Make sure to explain your response.

32 "Gift"

You are given $500 from the will of your late great uncle Rupert. In his will he instructs you to, "Save some, spend some, and give some." Be specific and explain what you will do with the money.

33 "Going to California"

What would it be like to know that you and your family were going to be moving to California in two weeks? What are some of the things you would want to do here before you left?

34 "Going to die"

Have you ever been close to death? If so, how did it make you feel? Do you think that coming close to dying makes a person wiser? Make sure to express what you think in your response.

35 "Growing up"

What is the most difficult thing about growing up? What are some of the easy parts about being a kid? Make sure to explain and defend your response.

36 "Jail"

In the American prison system we have over two million inmates. Why do you think so many people are locked up? Is something wrong with our justice system? Are parents and schools doing their jobs?

37 "Job"

Getting and keeping a good job is more difficult than ever before. Other than money, why is it important for a person to have work? Make sure to explain your response.

38 "Judge"

"You can't judge a book by its cover."
What do you think this statement means? Make sure to explain and defend your answer.

39 "Life"

What is the best thing about life? Is this something you can attain? Make sure to explain your response.

40 "Like me"

How do you know when a person likes you? What are some of the things you might do when you like another person? Can you always tell when a person likes you?

41 "Live without"

What is something or someone in your life that you don't think you could live without? Be specific and explain why this person or object is so important to you.

42 "Love"

What is love? Make sure to explain and defend your response.

43 "Make a difference"

What are some steps you could take that would ultimately make the world a better place for everyone? Do you think it is possible for one person to make a positive difference to a lot of people?

44 "Marijuana"

With the evolving laws in this country concerning marijuana a great deal of questions and confusion exist about this drug. What are some of your thoughts and/or concerns about the use of this drug? Should it be made legal? What types of regulations, if any, do you think should be made about this drug? Make sure to defend and explain your opinion in your response.

45 "Me"

Describe yourself as a person. What are you like? What are you all about? Who are you?

46 "Money"

Why do you think it is difficult for people to save money? What specifically can you do to save money for future things you may want? Make sure to give some specific examples.

47 "Nice to hear"

What is the nicest compliment your hear people say about you that makes you feel the happiest? Who might say it? Make sure to explain your answer.

48 "No one cares"

Have you ever had the feeling that nobody cares so why should I? When you are feeling this way what are some of the things you can do to help turn your attitude around?

49 "Occupation"

If you could decide today to do anything in life for an occupation what would it be? Why do you think this would be an interesting and rewarding type of job for you?

50 "Opposite sex"

What are some of the most frustrating things about members of the opposite sex? Make sure to express and defend your opinion in your response.

51 "Pet peeve"

What is something that ticks you off more than anything else? Why does this get you so upset? What could you do to not allow this to bother you so much?

52 "Pet"

In your opinion what is the best type of pet to have? What is it about this type of pet that makes it so special?

53 "Police"

What do you think it would be like to be a police officer? Do you think their jobs are easy or difficult? How do some people view the police?

54 "Poor"

Identify and write about some of the major problems people in this country face who are poor. How do you think these issues negatively affect the minds of students who come from households that are struggling financially?

55 "Popular music"

Why does popular music have such a large impact on cultural changes? How do you think popular music affects students your age? Make sure to defend and explain your opinion in your response.

56 "Popularity"

What might be some of the problems that famous people face every day? Would you like to be famous to the point that everyone in the country knows who you are?

57 "Positive role model"

Who is a person you look up to that is a positive role model? Why do you consider this person important? Make sure to explain and defend your answer.

58 "Possession"

What is the one material thing you treasure the most? How did you get this object? Make sure to explain why this is so important to you in your response.

59 "Pride"

What is something you have done in your life that you are proud of? Explain why this accomplishment has stuck with you.

60 "Regret"

What is something you have done that you have regretted? What can you do now so you won't make this type of mistake ever again? Make sure to explain your response.

61 "Religion"

Why do you think that religion is such an important part in the lives of many different cultures all over the planet? Make sure to explain your response.

62 "Season"

What is your favorite season of the year? Why is this time of the year special for you? Make sure to explain your response.

63 "Sick or hurt"

Tell about a time you were really sick or hurt. What happened to you? How long were you down and who took care of you? Be thorough and explain.

64 "Sleep"

Why do you think sleep is so important to a person's wellness? Do you get enough sleep? What could you do to get more? How do you think the lack of sleep negatively affect the minds of students?

65 "Smell"

The sense of smell is the greatest for triggering our memory. What is one of your favorite fragrances? Make sure to explain why this smell represents something good to you.

66 "Space"

Why do you think we explore space? Do you think exploring space is a good or bad idea? Make sure to be specific in your defense and explanation in your response.

67 "Sports or business"

Are professional sports games or just another type of business? Make sure to explain what your opinion is in your response.

68 "STD"

What can a person do to watch out for their own health? How do you think having an STD would negatively affect the thoughts of a student your age? Make sure to defend and explain your response.

69 "Stress"

What do you stress over the most? Why is stressing over this such a big deal to you?

70 "Stupid choices"

What is the number one reason people do stupid things? What might help us be better decision makers?

71 "Success"

What are some typical characteristics of a successful person? Who do you view in life as being successful? What do you think is the key to their success? Please explain your response.

72 "Teens working"

Should teenagers have jobs? How do you think working as a teen affects the minds and schedules of students? Make sure to defend your stance by supporting your view.

73 "Temper"

What do you think is the worst thing about having a reputation for losing your temper? How do you think people would think of you if you were always getting into fights and could not control yourself?

74 "Top 10 things to do"

What are the top 10 things you would like to do in your life before you die? Number 1-10 and make you list.

75 "True hero"

What are some of the qualities that make a person a true hero? Who do you consider to be a true hero and not just a flashy idol? Make sure to explain your response.

76 "TV Show"

If you could make and star in your own TV show that millions would see, what would it be about? Make sure to explain your response.

77 "TV viewing"

What was your favorite thing to watch on TV when you were 6 years old? What is your favorite thing to watch on TV now? Explain how your taste in shows has changed over the years.

78 "Vandalism"

What do you consider to be vandalism? Explain how vandalism hurts people. Have you or your family ever been vandalized?

79 "Video games"

Statistics show that some students play video games 5 or more hours a day. How do you think this may negatively affect the minds of these students?

80 "What you don't know..."

Explain the following statement:
"What you don't know can't hurt you."
Do you think this is true? Make sure to defend your response.

81 "Who"

Who do you think has had the greatest impact on America in the last hundred years? Has this person had a negative or positive influence on this country? Can you recall some of the things this person has done that makes them important?

82 "Worst qualities"

Each of us has qualities about our personality that makes up who we are. What are the qualities about you that are the worst? Are you mean, dishonest, or jealous? What qualities about you are your weaknesses? Make sure to explain.

Questions concerning home and family

These questions can often bring out very personal feelings from students. Nothing strikes a chord louder than bringing up issues a student might be having at home. While these questions are not designed to push students towards unlocking deep seated issues they are experiencing at home, students will often reveal true concerns they are having with their living situations. If a student is struggling or refusing to write about one of these prompts I always let them tell me what they would like to write about and will typically go with their suggestion.

"The only thing that gets me annoyed at home is when my little brother won't leave me alone."

A line from a student's response to #11 - "Living with frustration"

Questions concerning home and family

1. Adoption
2. Advice about parents
3. Bad parent
4. Best vacation
5. Child abuse
6. Curfews
7. Funny thing
8. Good advice to parent
9. Good parent
10. Ideal weekend
11. Living with frustration
12. Old argument
13. Spoiled brat
14. Tell parent
15. Weekend
16. Where from

1 "Adoption"

What would you do if you found out that your parents adopted you when you were a baby? How might this make you feel? Do you think you would attempt to find out about your natural parents? Make sure to explain your response.

2 "Advice about parents"

A good friend's parents are getting a divorce and are fighting over child custody. What advice would you give your friend? Make sure to explain why you would give this advice.

3 "Bad Parent"

What are some things that parents do that negatively impacts their children? Why do you think this is so bad? Make sure to explain your answer.

4 "Best vacation"

What was the best time you ever had on a vacation? Where did you go? Who was there? How old were you? Be specific in your response.

5 "Child abuse"

Child abuse is a big problem in this country. What do you think can be done to stop child abuse? Make sure to give some specific solutions in your response.

6 "Curfews"

Do you think that having curfews for teens are a good idea? What do you think is an appropriate curfew time for someone your age? Make sure to defend and explain your opinion in your response.

7 "Funny thing"

Who in your family has the most sense of humor? What is the funniest thing one of your family members has ever done? Make sure to be specific in your response.

8 "Good advice to parents"

Many parents find it difficult to enjoy life and have fun. If you were to give them some advice about how to enjoy their lives more, what would you tell them? Make sure to explain your answer.

9 "Good parent"

What do you think are the most important things a parent can do to make sure their child turns out to be a good person? Make sure to explain your answer.

10 "Ideal weekend"

Describe what you think would be an ideal weekend with your parents. Make sure to explain your response.

11 "Living with frustration"

What is the most frustrating thing about the people you live with? What could you do that might make the situation better for everyone?

12 "Old argument"

Is there an old argument that you seem to have over and over again with your parents? What do you think you could do to stop this old argument in the future? Make sure to explain your response.

13 "Spoiled brat"

What do you think is the best way to deal with a three year old who is a spoiled brat? How do you use discipline without abusing the child? Make sure to explain and defend your response.

14 "Tell parent"

What would you really like to tell your parent or parents that you have never told them before? Why do you want to tell them this? Please explain.

15 "Weekend"

The weather this weekend is going to be great. What are some of the things you are going to do to take advantage of such good weather? What might you do that is fun outside this weekend? Make sure to be specific in your response.

16 "Where are you from?"

Everyone is from a different place. What are some of the unique things about where you are from that has helped to shape you as an individual? Start your writing today with: "I was born in. . ."

Questions that pose dilemmas

This is typically the section of questions that students struggle with the most. Students will often attempt to ask additional questions about these situations to help them start on their journals. Often when given these questions kids will want to engage in a discussion to help them sort through some of the ethical issues that they pose. I often allow for extra time for them to work through their thoughts.

Many of us act before we think, and this is especially true for young people. This section is important because it engages the students to think about potential consequences of their actions. Students are facing new ethical decisions almost daily. Unlike adults, who have had more years of experience to develop judgement and decision skills, young people are in the early stages of learning their boundaries of integrity. It is the hope that by posing these questions it will encourage them to explore their personal code of ethics and to decide on deeper thinking responses.

"I would choose Sue... If she gets the heart maybe she will care more and help her kids get through life."
Lines from a student's response to #26 - "Your choice"

Questions that pose dilemmas

1. Animals
2. Blame
3. Car not starting
4. Corporal punishment
5. Crash
6. Dead
7. Death penalty
8. Drinking age
9. Energy drinks
10. Faces
11. Free
12. Gun
13. Job choices
14. Lost money
15. Make a wish
16. Mind or body
17. Operation
18. Philanthropy
19. Restroom find
20. Robbery
21. Soap opera
22. Theft
23. View a crime
24. Wallet
25. Wrong change
26. Your choice

1 "Animals"

Are humans animals? Please explain and defend your answer by providing a basis for what you believe.

2 "Blame"

Is following a true statement?
"The only person to blame is yourself."
Make sure to defend and explain your response.

3 "Car not starting"

You leave your job alone at night. It is winter and your car will not start. No one is around and you are in a bad part of town. You reach for your phone to make a call and realize that your battery is dead. What are you going to do to get yourself out of this situation? Make sure to be specific in your response.

4 "Corporal punishment"

Should corporal punishment be allowed in schools? Why or why not? Make sure to explain your response with support of your point of view.

5 "Crash"

Your plane crashes on an uninhabited island. What teacher would you pick to be stranded with? Remember your survival might depend on who you pick. Make sure to explain and defend your response.

6 "Dead"

What happens to you when you die? Make sure to explain and defend what you believe in your response.

7 "Death penalty"

Should the death penalty be made illegal in this country? What are some of the reasons you think we should or shouldn't have the death penalty? Make sure to explain and support your response.

8 "Drinking age"

Should the drinking age be changed? What age do you think people in this country should legally be allowed to drink? How do you think a change in the drinking age might affect the minds of students? Make sure to defend your stance by supporting your opinion.

9 "Energy drinks"

Should energy drinks be banned? Should they have a warning label on them, or perhaps an age requirement? How do you think energy drinks could affect the minds of students? Make sure to express your opinion on this issue in your response.

10 "Faces"

How do you act differently around your friends compared to an older person you have a lot of respect for? Make sure to be specific in explaining the type of ways you act different in your response.

11 "Free"

Explain the following statement:
"The best things in life are free."
Do you think this is a true statement? Why or why not? Make sure to explain and defend your response.

12 "Gun"

You catch a glimpse of a gun in a locker and overhear the owner say, *"I'm gonna get that guy!"* You are not sure if he saw you. What would you do? What might be the result of your action or your inaction? In your response make sure to defend what you would do.

13 "Job choices"

Would you rather have a job that paid you a lot but you hated, or a job you absolutely loved but barely paid you enough to make ends meet? Make sure to explain and defend the job choice you picked.

14 "Lost money"

Your parents give you $300 to deposit in the bank. You end up losing the money on the way to the bank. How are you going to deal with this situation? Make sure to defend and explain your actions.

15 "Make a wish"

The Make a Wish Foundation grants wishes to young people who are dying from diseases. Vacations, new cars, and meeting famous people are what many terminal youths have asked for in the past. One boy's wish was to hunt and kill an endangered bear. What would you tell this boy if you were the person deciding on his wish? Remember… this is his last wish.

16 "Mind or body"

When you get old would you rather have a body that works fine and a mind that doesn't, or a body that is broken and a sharp mind? Make sure to defend and explain your opinion in your response.

17 "Operation"

Your favorite pet, Ziggy, needs an operation. The cost is $975. You know your parents can't afford this. What would your input be in making the decision of what to do? Please explain your feelings of what to do with this 12 year old pet.

18 "Philanthropy"

You are so rich that your family and friends are set forever. You have so much money that you decide to give some away. What types of charity groups would you give your money to? Be specific and explain how you would go about helping others.

19 "Restroom find"

You just got a pass from class to go to the restroom. As you walk in the restroom you see a pistol on the counter next to the sink. No one is around. What do you do? Be specific and explain exactly how you would respond to this situation.

20 "Robbery"

Your parents are away for the weekend and you are to take care of the house by yourself. You go to sleep, but at 3:22 you get woken up because you hear someone in the kitchen. They may be robbing your house. What are you going to do? Make sure to be specific in your explanation of your actions.

21 "Soap opera"

You know a girl at school who is pregnant and claims the father is someone who really isn't the one. She picks this boy because she feels he will be a better father than the one who is the real boy. The real boy is an abusive person and a bully. She plans to have the child. The boys involved don't know, but you find out the truth. The pregnant girl doesn't know that you are aware of her secret. What do you do about this? Be specific and explain your actions.

22 "Theft"

What would you do if you found out someone had stolen a great deal of money from another student at school? Explain how you would view the thief now that you know they steal.

23 "View a crime"

You see some guy in a small locally owned store steal a watch. What do you do about this situation? Make sure to explain your reasons for action or in action.

24 "Wallet"

It's your mom's birthday today and you have only $10 to spend. You go to the mall to look for a gift and as you are walking in the parking lot you find a wallet and discover it has $300 in it. You are so excited you spend it all on your mom's gift. When you get home and are wrapping the present you take the time and look in the wallet again. You see an ID that belongs to your best friend's mom who you happen to know has just recently been laid off from her job. Make sure to explain what you are going to do.

25 "Wrong change"

You buy a soda from a local convenience store and give the cashier a $10 bill to pay for a $1.69 drink. Instead of returning $8.31 the clerk makes a mistake and gives you $18.31. What do you do? Please be specific and justify your reasoning for your decision.

26 "Your choice"

You are the person who decides who receives a heart transplant. There are three candidates that are your choices. The two people who don't get the heart will die within a few days. Make sure to support and defend your decision of who should receive the heart and live.

<u>Little Billy</u>: Little Billy is a ten year old with multiple health problems. He is extremely bright and considered gifted beyond most. Because of his ability he is already in the 9th grade.

<u>Community Ray</u>: Ray is the most recognized businessman in his small community of Four Falls, Montana. He gives to dozens of charitable organizations, including: the town park, new daycare center, and for starting the MR program – Minorities Read. He is 32, married, and father of three kids.

<u>Sue Single Mom</u>: Sue is a 17 year old single mother of two and a high school dropout. She's an OK mom, but she smokes and doesn't always make the best decisions. Due to her lack of education she might never have a good job.

Questions that are school related

One thing that kids like to write about is what is going on around them. This section is designed to tap into common topics related to school. Perhaps there is no section of writing prompts in this book that kids enjoy more than this one. Writers are taught to write about things they know about, so kids seem to really enjoy many of the questions from this section. Some of the strongest opinions are expressed from these prompts. Anytime students can relate to issues that affect them it helps to inspire their writing because they are more inclined to express what they truly think.

"It would probably be very boring if we didn't have school."
A line from a student's response to #8 - "No school"

Questions that are school related

1. Advice to a friend
2. Boys or girls
3. College
4. Diploma
5. Don't get it
6. Failure
7. Favorite class
8. My rules
9. No school
10. Pick tour teacher
11. School learning
12. School subject
13. School uniforms
14. Secret
15. Senior
16. Snacks and sodas
17. Snow days
18. Teacher
19. Graduate

1 "Advice to friend"

One of your best friends is starting to hang out with someone you feel is completely wrong for them. You and your other friends feel that this person is making a big mistake. What are you going to do? Please explain and defend why you might speak to your friend, or why you will decide to remain silent on this issue.

2 "Boys or girls"

Do you think boys or girls have it easier in school? Can you give examples to justify your response? Make sure to explain and defend your answer.

3 "College"

What do you think college might be like? Do you hope to go one day? Where might you go and what might you study? Make sure to explain your response.

4 "Diploma"

What does getting a high school diploma mean to you? Why is getting your diploma important? What does getting a high school diploma represent? Make sure to explain your response.

5 "Don't get it"

When you don't really understand something are you afraid to ask questions, or are you the type of person that will seek answers before you attempt to figure something out on your own? Make sure to explain your response by giving an example of how you approach something you don't get.

6 "Failure"

What is your greatest fear about failing in life? What can you do to avoid being a failure? Make sure to explain your response.

7 "Favorite class"

What has been your favorite class ever? Who was your teacher? Make sure to explain in your response why you picked this class as your all-time favorite.

8 "My rules"

List 3 new rules that you think would help the school run better. Will these rules make school a better place for learning? Make sure to defend each of your rules in your response.

9 "No school"

What would your life be like if you never had to go to school? What types of things do you think you would miss if you didn't get to go to school? Be sure to explain and defend your response.

10 "Pick your teacher"

Pick your teacher from the following:
a) A strict no nonsense teacher who is hard but teaches you well.
b) A teacher who is a lot of fun but doesn't teach you a whole lot.
Make sure to explain and defend the teacher you pick.

11 "School learning"

What do you consider the most important thing you have learned in school? Is this something you can take with you the rest of your life? Make sure to explain why this is important to you in your response.

12 "School subject"

Which subject in school do you think will be the most useful to your future? Why do you consider this subject to be important? Make sure to explain and defend your response.

13 "School uniforms"

Do you think that if your school system voted to have school uniforms it would be a good idea? In your response please state the pros and cons of going to a standardized uniform dress code for all students.

14 "Secret"

You just found out a juicy secret about someone at school. This person told you not to tell anyone. Would you tell someone this secret or not? Make sure to explain your response.

15 "Senior"

What do you think are some of the best things about being a senior? What do you hope for *your* senior year in high school? Make sure to explain your answer.

16 "Snacks and sodas"

Should snack and soda machines be taken out of all public schools? State your stance on this issue by giving three reasons why snacks and soda machines should or should not be allowed in school. Make sure to defend your responses.

17 "Snow day"

With winter in full swing it is highly possible that we may have a snow day soon. What is your favorite outdoor activity on days when school is cancelled? Please explain what you have done outside on previous snow days.

18 "Teacher"

If you were a teacher what would be some of your concerns? Do you think it would be easy or difficult to be an educator? Make sure to explain and defend your response.

19 "What I need to do before I graduate"

List the things you have to do before you graduate. Do you have all your credits? Have you passed all your standardized tests? What do you need to do to maintain your GPA and have a successful semester? Be specific in your list.

Questions that are fantasies

Students seem to enjoy this section because it gives them the opportunity to think beyond their typical lives of reality and explore their realms of possibilities. Having students think in terms of "what-ifs" gives them a chance to be creative in abstract ways that inspires innovations of thought. Many of the more nontraditional thinkers enjoy this section because the genre of fantasy is more akin to their tastes of expression. For the more conservative thinking students, this section gives them a chance to step outside of their comfort zones and begin to explore different ways of approaching issues.

"I've always wanted to go on an African safari and help the people there. I've always wanted to make them happy and give them what we have."

Lines from a student's response to #4 - "Big adventure"

Questions that are fantasies

1. 10 Years
2. 100
3. Army
4. Big adventure
5. Big storm
6. Big talk
7. Blind
8. Cat
9. Celebrity interest
10. Change
11. Choices
12. Different look
13. Dinner time
14. Dream house
15. Dream machine
16. England
17. Go anywhere
18. Heads up
19. Helping out
20. Invisible
21. Last meal
22. Movie star
23. Murder
24. Musical instrument
25. New job
26. New parent
27. New way
28. No diseases

29. No money
30. No parents
31. Olympic fall
32. One month
33. One wish
34. Other shoe
35. Out to eat
36. Rich
37. Sing, sing, sing
38. Star
39. Stuck
40. Time machine
41. Which one

1 "10 Years"

Where do you see yourself in ten years? What type of career, family, and personal goals do you think you will meet by then? Be specific in your response.

2 "100"

What do you think it would be like to be 100 years old? What would be some of the advantages and disadvantages to being 100? Make sure to explain your answer.

3 "Army"

You have been drafted in the army and are to report to boot camp in Oklahoma in two weeks. What are some of your concerns and questions about having to join the military? How do you think this may affect you and your family? Make sure to explain your response.

4 "Big adventure"

What big adventure would you like to have in your life? What is something you always wanted to do? It may be a trip or a vacation. It could be a place you would like to live or a lifestyle you see yourself in. What is your big adventure? Start your writing with: *"I always wanted to. . ."*

5 "Big storm"

The following occurs:
At six o'clock this evening a big storm causes all power to go out in the county. At the same time everyone's internet and cell phone services fail as well. What do you think the impact will be on you and your family? Please be sure to explain what you would do.

6 "Big talk"

If you had a half hour to talk to the president what would you have to say to him? What are some of the questions you would like to ask the president if you had a one on one meeting with him? Make sure to explain your response.

7 "Blind"

How would your life change if you woke up tomorrow morning and discovered that you couldn't see? What types of things would become drastically different? Make sure to explain your answer by giving specific examples.

8 "Cat"

What do you think it would be like to be a cat for a week? What type of adventures might you have as a cat? Make sure to provide details in your response.

9 "Celebrity interest"

What celebrity are you interested in? How long have you known about this person? Make sure to be specific when explaining why you picked this person.

10 "Change"

No one is perfect! If you could change one thing about yourself what would it be? Is this a physical change or a personality change? Make sure to explain in your response how you think this change might make you feel.

11 "Choices"

If you could have either the ability to talk to animals or the power to read the minds of others, which would you want? Make sure to explain and defend your choice.

12 "Different look"

What do you think it would be like to be a different race for a week? How do you think that by being a member of another race it might open your eyes to different things? Make sure to explain what you think you might discover.

13 "Dinner time"

If you could have dinner with three people living or dead who would they be? Individually explain why you picked each of these dinner guests.

14 "Dream house"

Have you ever thought about your dream house? Describe in detail some of the things that would be in your dream house. Also, describe where you would like your dream house to be located. Make sure to be specific in your response.

15 "Dream machine"

What would be your dream vehicle to own? What would it feel like to have exactly what you wanted? What would be some of the responsibilities with owning this vehicle? Make sure to explain.

16 "England"

You have a chance to live in England for an entire school year with a distant cousin. You wouldn't be able to see your family or friends for close to a year. Would you go or stay home? Make sure to explain and defend your response.

17 "Go anywhere"

Imagine you could go anywhere on earth. Where would you go and what would you do there? In your response make sure to be specific in your reasons for picking this place to go.

18 "Heads up"

What would you do if the news told us that on Saturday a large group of meteors were going to hit the planet? Make sure to be specific in your response.

19 "Helping out"

What sort of things could you do to earn money if your parents lost their jobs and you wanted to help out with the financial support of your family? Please be sure explain how being in this situation might affect you.

20 "Invisible"

What would you do if you could be invisible for three days? Make sure to explain and defend your actions during this three day period.

21 "Last meal"

People waiting to be executed are often given anything they want to eat for their last meal. What would you order if you could have anything you wanted for your last meal? Make sure to include drink and dessert. (Hopefully you will never have to make this real decision.) Make sure to explain why you picked the foods you ordered.

22 "Movie star"

If you were a star in a movie what type of movie would you be in? Who would you like to have in the movie as a co-star? Make sure to explain why you would pick this type of film to star in.

23 "Murder"

What would you do if you found out your favorite teacher or coach had killed someone ten years ago? Make sure to defend and explain your response.

24 "Musical instrument"

If you could play any type of musical instrument what would it be? Can you play anything now? Explain the reason why you picked this instrument.

25 "New job"

What do you think it would be like to be your parents for a week? Make sure to explain your response.

26 "New parent"

How would your life change if you became a parent at 17? What do you think would be some of your new responsibilities if you became a parent at this age? Make sure to explain your response.

27 "New way"

How would your life be different if you lost the ability to walk? How do you think this may affect your success at school? Make sure to explain your response.

28 "No diseases"

What do you think life would be like if there were no diseases? What would be the good and bad side of a world with no diseases? Make sure to explain and defend your response.

29 "No money"

Your family suddenly lost all the money they had including their jobs. What might change in your life? How might you be able to help? Make sure to explain your answer.

30 "No parents"

What would you do if you were in charge of your house for an entire weekend and no adults were around? Make sure to be specific in what you would do.

31 "Olympic fall"

How would you feel if you fell at the Olympic Games? Would you continue with the race or performance, or would you give up? Make sure to explain and defend your decision in your response.

32 "One month"

How would you live your life if you knew you only had a month to live? What are some of the things you would like to do with your remaining time? Make sure to be specific in your response.

33 "One wish"

If you were granted one wish, other than money or other wishes, what would you wish for? Is this wish possible for you to attain on your own? Make sure to explain why you picked this wish in your response.

34 "Other shoe"

What would it be like to be a member of the opposite sex for a week? What are some of the things you think you might discover? Make sure to explain your response.

35 "Out to eat"

Where would you go if you could take your entire family out to eat to any restaurant? What would you order off the menu? Have you ever been to this place before? Please explain.

36 "Rich"

How could being extremely rich change you as a person? What types of things would be different in your life if you were extremely rich? Make sure to explain your response.

37 "Sing, sing, sing"

You have been selected to be on a TV voice competition. What song will you sing in front of a TV audience of millions? Explain why you picked this song to sing? What significance does this song have to you? Make sure to explain your response.

38 "Star"

What do you think the life of a music star would be like? How do you think you would handle the attention if you were a music star? Make sure to explain your answer.

39 "Stuck"

You are stuck by yourself on a remote island that has electricity but only a TV and a DVD/CD player that work. No phone or internet service? You are able to take music from 5 musicians. You can take 5 movies. You can take 3 tools. Make your three lists.

40 "Time machine"

Where would you go if you could travel to any place in time and come back today? Why did you pick this place in time? What do you think this time might be like?

41 "Which one"

Would you rather be a wealthy and famous musician or a scientist that does research that helps sick people but who is not famous or rich? Make sure to explain and defend your choice in your response.

Questions during holidays or big events

These questions are typically easy and fun for students to answer. They are usually a nice break from some of the more challenging questions that kids sometimes have troubles with. Students will usually write longer on the majority of these questions because they have a good deal of prior knowledge about these topics. Generally these prompts are nice reminders of things that students enjoy and look forward to, so getting solid and quick responses are typical.

However, some students who struggle with being out of the routine of school might have a hard time going into the longer breaks of the school year. For students who are experiencing issues at home these questions might bring out concerns and anxieties they are having about the time spent being away from school.

"...wondering if you're gonna get your heart broken or not. Also, knowing that you're gonna marry them or break up is nerve racking."
Lines from a student's response to #11 - "Love stinks"

Questions during holidays or big events

1. 1st Quarter
2. Earth Day
3. Flu season
4. Halloween
5. Love is great
6. Love stinks
7. New year – New you
8. New Year's resolutions
9. New Year
10. Reflections
11. Spring break
12. Spring
13. Super Bowl
14. Thankful
15. Time change
16. Vote
17. Wild turkey
18. Winter break fun
19. Winter break

1 "1st Quarter"

You have completed ¼ of the school year. What can you do to build on your success to do even better this next quarter? Make sure to be specific in your response.

2 "Earth Day"

Number your paper 1-7. What are seven specific things you can do to help the planet? Make sure to be specific with each of your responses.

3 "Flu season"

This year flu season is already on us. Some experts say this may be the worst flu season ever. List 7 things you can do to help you avoid getting the flu and staying healthy.

4 "Halloween"

What was your best Halloween costume ever? How old were you? Who was with you during that Halloween? Make sure to explain some details about this memory in your response.

5 "Love is great"

What do you think are some of the best things about loving someone? Make sure to only explain the good side of being in love.

6 "Love stinks"

What do you think are some of the worst things about loving someone? Make sure to only explain the bad side of being in love.

7 "New year – New you"

Name something you would like to see change for the better this year. Why do you want to see this change happen? What will you have to do to help the change occur? Be specific for each point.

8 "New Year's resolutions"

Please number your paper 1-5 and list 5 academic resolutions you want to achieve by the end of this semester. By each resolution specifically tell me what you will have to do to achieve this. Make sure the resolutions you pick can be reached.

9 "New Year"

Welcome back! What are three aspects of your life that you would like to see change for the better this year? For each one explain something you will need to do to help the change occur. Please be specific.

10 "Reflection"

You are half way through the school year! In what ways has this half year been successful for you? What are some things you could improve upon for the second half of the year? Make sure to explain your response.

11 "Spring break"

For the next several days we don't have school. What are some of the fun things you hope to do during your break? Make sure to be specific in your response.

12 "Spring"

The weather is finally turning nice. Spring is in the air. What is it about this season that so many people seem to enjoy? What are your favorite things about this season? Make sure to be specific in your answer.

13 "Super Bowl"

Why do you think our culture puts so much importance on the Super Bowl? Do you consider this an important yearly event? Make sure to explain and defend your response.

14 "Thankful"

What are seven things you are thankful for? Number 1-7 – give yourself space between each number - and list things you are thankful for. Specifically explain why you are thankful for each of the seven things you listed.

15 "Time change"

This weekend we'll need to set our clocks forward by one hour. How will having an extra hour of sunlight at the end of each day affect you? How do you view this time change? Remember, it will be much darker in the morning. Make sure to defend and explain your opinion in your response.

16 "Vote"

Why do you think people vote? When you turn 18 do you plan to vote in elections? Please be specific and explain why you will or why you may not vote in the future.

---

17 "Wild turkey"

You are a wild turkey! What is the holiday season is like for you? Remember to write this from the perspective of the turkey.

18 "Winter break fun"

What is something you did the last two weeks that was fun? Did you go anywhere? What was the best part of your break? Make sure to explain in your response.

19 "Winter break"

We are about to have several days away from classes. Other than sleep, what are some of the things you want to do with all the time you will have during this break from school? Make sure to be specific in your response.

Questions for the end of the school year

At the end of each school year I give my students writing prompts to help them think about the summer and to reflect on the past school year. Hopefully students have experienced some successes and these prompts give them an opportunity to write about their accomplishments and future goals. I have found that students do take a good deal of pride being promoted to the next grade level. These prompts are designed to address the things they did right to allow them to move forward in school. These prompts also are also geared towards the anticipation of the summer months that are soon to come. For students who have not had a good year these writing prompts can be difficult because it just reminds them of what could have been accomplished if they had applied themselves.

"If I focus and work harder I most definitely think I will be okay."
A line from a student's response to #1 - "9 to go"

Questions for the end of school year

1. 9 to go
2. Final pull
3. Goals for next year
4. Next year
5. Looking back
6. Summer plans

1 "9 to go"

This school year has 9 weeks remaining. You have many things to accomplish before the end of the school year. What are your specific educational goals for finishing out the year? Please make a list of ten specific things you need to do to finish the year successfully.

2 "Final pull"

How would you like to see the rest of the school year go for you? Do you think you will be able to achieve your academic goals by the end of the year? How do you plan to get to where you want to be?

3 "Goals for next year"

This year is almost over. Hopefully you reached many of your goals that you listed from the very first journal entry. List 5 goals for next school year that you hope to achieve.

4 "Looking back"

Looking back over the last nine months of this school year many good and bad things have happened. What have been some of your successes? Do you have any regrets from this past year? Make sure to be specific in your response.

5 "Next year"

What do you think next year will be like for you in school? Do you think you will be taking harder classes? Will you be working as well as going to school? What do you expect next year will be like? Make sure to explain your thoughts in your response.

6 "Summer plans"

What are some of your plans for this summer? Are you taking a trip? Are you going to be working? What are some of the things you hope to do this summer? Please explain in your response.

Closing Thoughts

Starting off class with a question really seems to set the tone that *our* classroom is a place of learning. These questions serve as signals to my students that our class is a place where their thoughts are going to be challenged and they are going to be asked to think. With today's instant access to information children have a tendency to go to their phones or other devices to find answers rather than thinking about possible solutions to difficult questions. The ability to think critically and develop problem solving skills seem to be lacking in many young people's approach towards finding answers to questions. This collection of questions is an attempt to pose intriguing and often complex issues to students that persuade them to think and respond through challenging their creative, ethical, and thought provoking skills.

Teachers are constantly attempting to develop challenging lessons that get kids to think. I hope this collection of questions can help the many teachers that struggle daily to find different ways to engage their students to think critically while at the same time help to create ways in which positive connections can be fostered.

Finding out what their kids are thinking is often what parents seem to wonder about. I hope this book can help parents discover a bit of insight into what is going on with their kids' thoughts and how their children approach different ways of answering complex questions

J.D.

Acknowledgments

"When you practice gratefulness, there is a sense of respect toward others."

Dalai Lama

Many people have helped with seeing this book come to print. I am thankful to Dave Ridenour and Patricia L'Herrou, for their editing help and wonderful words of encouragement. I'm thankful to my colleagues at work who took the time to read the book and write nice reviews. These educators include: John Ringstaff, Chris Garland, and Mary Lisker. A big thanks to my good friend and historian/educator Christian Cotz for his wonder review. Michelle Martin is a wiz on computers and was very helpful on technical formatting as well as reviewing the book – thank you. For letting me bend an ear on many issues, I'm thankful for my longtime friend and fellow teacher Mark Hopkins, who is always a phone call away. A huge thank you to my publisher, Douglas Dollar and the good people at New Forums Press for the many things that they do. My wife, Maile L'Herrou, who gives me her honest opinions and who is always helpful and encouraging – thank you. Lastly, I'm thankful to my students who, through their successes and failures, have inspired this book.

Many Thanks, JD

About the Author

Joe Deely graduated with a Masters in Education degree from James Madison University in 1995 and started teaching that fall. He has taught students in grades 6 through 12 his entire 23 year career in public schools.

As an alternative education teacher, he finds that his students often struggle with academic, social, and emotional difficulties. His specialty is teaching kids who have a hard time understanding what to do to be successful at school.

"Getting kids to answer questions is fairly easy," He notes, adding, "Getting them to think about the question before they answer is tricky."

Deely is also the author of *Hints for Success in School: A Practical Guide for Students*, published in 2017 by New Forums Press.

23069936R00059

Made in the USA
Columbia, SC
07 August 2018